Reading for Today

A Sequential **5** Program for Adults

Program Authors	Jim Beers
	Linda Ward Beech
	Tara McCarthy
	Sam V. Dauzat
	Jo Ann Dauzat
Teacher's Edition Author	Norman Najimy
Program Consultant	Donna Amstutz
Program Advisors	Lonnie Farrell
	Aryola Taylor
	Adriana Figueroa
	Carol Paggi
	Jean Batey
	Ann Reed
	Sharon Darling
	Susan Paull

STECK-VAUGHN
C O M P A N Y
A Subsidiary of National Education Corporation

Acknowledgements

Photography:
Jim Myers—cover
Sandy Wilson—iv, 9, 70, 79
Mike Flahive—14, 23, 56–57, 65, 66–67
Rick Patrick—29, 37, 42, 51, 84
David E. Kennedy—93

Print:
The TV schedule on page 55 is reprinted with
permission from *TV GUIDE*® Magazine, copyright
© 1986 by Triangle Publications, Inc., Radnor,
Pennsylvania.

Table of Contents

Buying on Time

Ray and Star Pope went shopping to look for a new bedroom set.

"Look, Ray," said Star, "that one is cute, don't you think? It looks like it's made of pine."

Ray wanted his wife to buy what she liked, but they did not make much money. "I bet that set costs a lot, Star," he said.

"Let's go ask how much it is," Star said as she led Ray into the store.

Ray put out his hand and said, "Hold on, Star. Before we buy anything, let's think about it. Don't forget that we have two big bills to pay right now."

Star laughed and gave Ray a hug. "We'll find a way," she said. "These stores let you buy on time, so we could pay bit by bit."

Review Words

A. Check the words you know.

☐ 1. save   ☐ 2. spend   ☐ 3. pregnant
☐ 4. cost   ☐ 5. piano   ☐ 6. company
☐ 7. wife   ☐ 8. bring   ☐ 9. straight
☐ 10. baby   ☐ 11. coupon   ☐ 12. customer

B. Read and write these sentences.

1. Ray and his wife can't spend much money.

2. They need some straight talk about cost.

3. Star is pregnant, and she will be glad when she can bring the baby to see her parents.

4. The Popes need to shop with a good company.

C. Choose an answer from the words in the list.

1. something to play music on _____

2. a person who shops in a store _____

3. something to save you money _____

4. to put money away _____

Sight Words

furniture   little   afford   so

▶ The Popes could not <u>afford</u> a lot of <u>furniture</u> because they had <u>so</u> <u>little</u> money, and a baby was coming.

A. Read the sight words above and the example sentence. Underline the sight words in 1—5.

1. The Popes needed furniture, so they went shopping.
2. They could not afford to spend much money.
3. They had saved a little money for furniture.
4. Many furniture sets cost so much that the Popes could not afford them.
5. They hoped to get the furniture and pay a little bit at a time.

B. Choose the words below to finish the sentences.

little   so   furniture   afford

1. Star wanted a big bed and a _____ table.
2. "Can we _____ to buy both of them?" she asked.
3. "I hope _____," said Ray, "we need them."
4. "Our home will look better with some new _____."

C. Read the sentences. Underline the sight words.

Star and Ray wanted to forget about saving money when they saw the furniture they wanted. They liked it so much that they did not want to think about cost. But they could not afford all the furniture at once. Can they buy it a little at a time?

Sight Words

pretty   credit   check   name

▶ The store does a <u>pretty</u> good <u>credit</u> <u>check</u> on your <u>name</u>.

A. Read the sight words above and the example sentence. Underline the sight words in 1—5.

1. Star liked the pine set because it was pretty.

2. "Can a customer get credit here?" asked Star.

3. Mr. Silva, who worked in the store, took Ray's and Star's names.

4. Mr. Silva ran a credit check on them.

5. "I checked, and your credit is pretty good," he told them.

B. Choose the words below to finish the sentences.

name   check   pretty   credit

1. The Popes have good _____ because they pay bills on time.

2. They do _____ well with the pay they get.

3. They try to _____ how much they spend.

4. Customers need to keep a good _____ with stores.

C. Read the sentences. Underline the sight words.

Ray and Star wanted to buy some pretty furniture before the baby came. They checked some ads to see about how much a bedroom set would cost. Ray and Star might have to buy the furniture on credit. They had a good name with credit companies because they pay bills on time.

Sight Words

yes   plain   month   interest

▶ Could the Popes pay a little every <u>month</u>? <u>Yes</u>, but it is <u>plain</u> that they would pay <u>interest</u>, too.

A. Read the sight words above and the example sentences. Underline the sight words in 1—3.

1. "Will the bedroom set cost more if we pay month by month?" Star asked.

2. "Yes," said Ray. "It is plain that it will cost more if we buy on time."

3. "That is because you will be paying interest every month," Mr. Silva said.

B. Choose the words below to finish the sentences.

month   yes   interest   plain

1. It was _____ to see that Star and Ray wanted the bedroom set.

2. "Will you like paying for it _____ by _____?" Star asked Ray.

3. "_____," he said, "that's OK with me."

4. "I want to check on the _____ rates in other stores before we make up our minds," said Star.

C. Read the sentences. Underline the sight words.

"Do you like this plain bedroom set?" Ray asked. "Yes," Star said, "but I've been thinking of a pretty one for months." Could they afford it? Ray and Star were trying to be responsible about money. They always used coupons when they shopped. They did not want to get into trouble over heavy interest.

Phonics: *-ain* and *-ame*

---

plain
gain
main
pain
rain

A. Read the words in the box. Make more *-ain* words.

br + ain = _____

ch + ain = _____

st + ain = _____

str + ain = _____

B. Write an *-ain* word to finish each sentence.

1. Ray liked the pine table, but it had a bad

   _____ on it.

2. A new bed was the _____ thing they needed.

3. Buying the furniture on credit would not put a

   _____ on the Popes.

---

name
came
game
same

A. Read the words in the box. Make more *-ame* words.

bl + ame = _____

fr + ame = _____

sh + ame = _____

B. Write an *-ame* word to finish each sentence.

1. It's a _____ that the table has a stain.

2. A store down the street has the _____ pine furniture.

3. No one would _____ us if we got the table there.

Phonics: Long *a*

A. The letters *ai, ay,* and *a-e* can all stand for the long *a* sound. Listen for the vowel sound in each word below. Underline the letters that stand for the long *a* sound.

ai	ay	a-e
plain	day	age
pain	pay	name
paid	play	make

B. Make other long *a* words below. Read and write the words.

-aid

m + aid = _____

r + aid = _____

br + aid = _____

-ay

w + ay = _____

st + ay = _____

gr + ay = _____

-age

p + age = _____

w + age = _____

st + age = _____

-ape

dr + ape = _____

gr + ape = _____

sh + ape = _____

C. Write *ai* or *ay* or *a-e* to make words below.

1. Star likes the sh_p_ of this pine table.

2. This set will look good with the dr_p_s.

3. Ray likes the pl__n black table.

4. Star likes the blue and gr__ set better.

Comparisons

small   smaller than   smallest

We add the endings -er and -est to some words to compare things.

A. Add each ending to write the new words.

	Add -er	**Add -est**
1. old	_____	_____
2. straight	_____	_____
3. neat	_____	_____
4. long	_____	_____
5. tight	_____	_____
6. clean	_____	_____

B. Practice reading the paragraph. Underline the words that compare things.

"This is a long table, but I want a longer one," said Ray. "My sister has the longest table in the family. We can all sit at that table."

"Our older table will have to do for now. Our money will be tighter when we buy a bedroom set."

C. Write the words below in the sentences.

smaller   longest   cleanest

1. We have been in many stores. Some are clean,

   but this is the _____ store we have seen.

2. This rug is too big. Can we find one that is

   _____?

3. I want a long table. Is this the _____ table you have?

The Chance of a Lifetime?

How can Ray and Star get the furniture they want?

Star ran over to the pine bedroom set. She sat on the big bed and looked at the little end tables and the two lights.

Mr. Silva, the man who had checked Ray's and Star's credit, came right over when he saw Star's interest in the set.

"Isn't that a pretty little set?" he said. "I think it's the cutest one in the store, and what a good buy! You can have it for $800."

—Chance—

Mr. Silva walked around the bedroom set talking all the time. There was something fake about him. He said things like *credit, no money down,* and *big savings.* But he didn't talk about interest rates. Pretty soon he took out his pad and made out a bill.

"We can get the bedroom set to you today if you put your names here now," he said with a wink at Star.

"Hold on there," said Ray. "My wife and I need time to think this over. We don't buy furniture every day, you know."

"Yes, this is a big event for us, so we want to check it all out," said Star.

Mr. Silva looked down. It was plain to see that these customers were going to take more of his time.

"Tell us about your interest rates," said Ray. "I know that if we buy on time, we'll pay more. If we take 18 months to pay for the furniture, how much interest will we pay?"

Mr. Silva laughed and said, "It's not so much, don't think about it. I know you can afford it, and you'll have the use of the bedroom set for so many more months."

"Yes, Mr. Silva, but how much money in interest are we talking about?" asked Star. "We know what the furniture costs, but what will the interest cost us?"

"I can see that you need to talk to my boss," said Mr. Silva. When it comes to a good buy, he'll give you the chance of a lifetime."

Star said, "I don't think we want to talk to your boss. I think we want to shop around some more. We want some straight talk about credit and interest rates. You're giving us the run-around."

Ray and Star walked out of the store.

—Chance—

Star and Ray looked some more. They didn't find any furniture that day. It took two months before they once again saw some bedroom furniture they wanted. It was at the Holiday Home Furniture Company. By then they had saved a little more money, and they could afford to put more money down. They could pay a bit more every month, so the bill would be paid sooner.

"I feel much better about this," said Star. "We are buying from a store with a good name, and we will be paying bills we can afford. I think we got a fine bedroom set, too."

Ray said, "Now that we've got the bedroom set, Star, I want to tell you about some more things I've been wanting for our home."

"Let's have it," Star said.

"Sit down," said Ray. "I want a camera, an AM/FM radio, a big TV set, a VCR player, a piano, and a newer car."

"You're a kick," said Star, "do you know that? Why don't you run right over to see Mr. Silva? His boss will give you the chance of a lifetime!"

Comprehension: Finding Facts

Tips for Finding Facts

Facts are small bits of information, like names, dates, or something that happened or that was said. What people think or feel about something is <u>not</u> a fact. To find facts in what you read, ask yourself:

- Who?
- Where?
- How much/many?
- What?
- When?

A. Find these facts in the story. Write the answers.

1. **Who** is Star? _____

2. **What** did Mr. Silva want to sell to the Popes?

   _____

3. **How much** money did Mr. Silva ask for the

   bedroom set? _____

4. **Where** did the Popes buy a bedroom set?

   _____

5. **When** did Ray tell Star what he wanted for the

   home? _____

B. Find these facts in the story. Write the words.

1. Star and Ray wanted a _____.

                                              rug   desk   bedroom set

2. After two _____, the Popes found a

               days   months   years

   bedroom set they liked.

3. By then, they had saved more _____.

                                         credit   money   furniture

Life Skill: Payment Schedule

payment	total	insurance

A. Read the new words. Then read the payment schedule below.

8/5/87

Payment Schedule

Unpaid balance	$800.00
Property Insurance	48.31
Life Insurance	12.08
Accident & Health Insurance	27.16
Non-Filing Insurance	10.00
Amount Financed	897.55
Finance Charge (@21%)	188.49
Total of Payments	1,086.04

APR (Annual Percentage Rate)   21%

First Payment Due	9/8/87
17 payments at	63.00
1 payment at	15.04

B. Read the questions and write the answers.

1. a. What is the total that the Popes will pay over 18 months? _____

   b. By taking 18 months to pay for an $800 bedroom set, how much more will the Popes pay? _____

2. a. When do the Popes need to make the first payment? _____

   b. How much is it? _____

   c. How much is the end payment? _____

3. What rate of interest will the Popes pay?

   _____

Looking Back

People on this block like to talk to Kate O'Dell. She has a friendly word for everyone she meets. Kate is my grandmother, and she's one of the oldest people around here. In our family, Kate's a star. She still thinks straight and talks straight. She named me Jean, after her mother.

Kate tells us about times that were different from our own times. She tells us about the old country she came from as a child. If you listen to Kate, it's like going back to an age we'll never see again.

Some of my brothers and sisters have no interest in hearing about the old days, but I love to listen to my grandmother. Over and over she tells me what it was like to be a foreigner in a new land. She tells of the long trip to this country.

"Times were bad in the old country," she says. "People hoped to get away from some bad problems. Well, they found that life here was no picnic at first. But we worked and made a better life in this new homeland."

"How did you meet Grandfather O'Dell?" I ask, and then I relax in my seat. I know I'll be here for a long time. Someday I'll tell my own grandchildren about the old days, and I'll tell them about Kate O'Dell, too.

Review Words

A. Check the words you know.

☐ 1. meet ☐ 2. still ☐ 3. foreign
☐ 4. over ☐ 5. away ☐ 6. grass
☐ 7. long ☐ 8. jump ☐ 9. picnic
☐ 10. new ☐ 11. park ☐ 12. snacks

B. Read and write these sentences.

1. Kate came over here from a faraway country.

_____

_____

2. She still likes to meet people from home.

_____

_____

3. For a long time, everything here was foreign and new to Kate.

_____

_____

4. Kate likes to walk in the grass in the park.

_____

_____

C. Read the clues. Complete the puzzle.

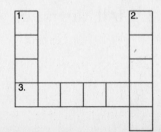

Down

1. a way to move fast
2. food that is quick to eat

Across

3. a party in a park

Sight Words

grandmother   their   only   farm

▶ My <u>grandmother</u> and her sister were the <u>only</u> ones to go away from <u>their</u> family's <u>farm</u>.

A. Read the sight words above and the example sentence. Underline the sight words in 1–4.

1. My grandmother was not an only child.
2. She and her brothers and sisters helped their parents on the farm in the old country.
3. The farm did not meet their needs.
4. My grandmother said the only thing to do was to find a home in a new country.

B. Choose the words below to finish the sentences.

only   their   farm   grandmother

1. Kate and her sister Nell did not want to go away from the _____, but they did.
2. Kate was _____ 16 years old at the time.
3. My _____ was so pretty at that age!
4. She and Nell were willing to take _____ chances on a better life in a new land.

C. Read the sentences. Underline the sight words.

Many of the farms in the old country did not have good land. My grandmother's family worked a long day, from sunup to sundown, but the farm could never feed 11 people. The parents saw some of their smaller children get sick. My grandmother's older brothers wanted to go to the city, but they only talked about it, and never did it.

Sight Words

---

price   live   wait   remember

▶ The longer I <u>live</u>, the more I <u>remember</u> that year. We had to <u>wait</u> to save for the <u>price</u> of a ticket.

A. Read the sight words above and the example sentences. Underline the sight words in 1—3.

1. Kate still remembers her long wait on the ship to get to a new land.

2. Kate and Nell had saved money to pay for the price of the trip.

3. The long wait on the ship was part of the price people paid to live in a new land.

B. Choose the words below to finish the sentences.

wait   live   price   remember

1. They paid a big _____ for a ticket.

2. I have to _____ that my grandmother's times were different from ours.

3. They had to _____ for years and save the money to go.

4. They had to _____ without many things.

C. Read the sentences. Underline the sight words.

My grandmother remembers her life as a child. The children had to work, but they waited for their chance to play.

"I've lived here a long time," says Kate, "but I would jump at the chance to see that old farm. I would pay a big price to go back again."

Sight Words

off   died   story   Ellis Island

▶ My grandmother tells the <u>story</u> of getting <u>off</u> the ship at <u>Ellis Island</u>. The sad part is that her sister Nell <u>died</u> on the trip over.

A. Read the sight words above and the example sentences. Underline the sight words in 1—3.

1. The story of the trip to Ellis Island is sad.
2. Nell was one of many who died on the ship.
3. Kate remembers getting off the ship at Ellis Island without her sister.

B. Choose the words below to finish the sentences.

story   Ellis Island   die   off

1. Kate could see the big city from _____ _____.

2. People listened to the life _____ and checked the health of every foreigner who came here.

3. Kate said, "I sometimes had the feeling that I would _____ from standing in lines for days."

4. After a time, Kate set _____ for the city.

C. Read the sentences. Underline the sight words.

My grandmother remembers the long days on Ellis Island where some people died. Many of them had been sick back in their old homes. Some of them got sick after they got off the ships.

"Ellis Island is part of the story of our country," Kate always says, "and the island is part of my story, too. I'm lucky that my story worked out as well as it did."

Phonics: -*ie* and -*ice*

---

die
pie
vie

A. Read the words in the box. Make other -*ie* words.

l + ie = _____

t + ie = _____

B. Write an -*ie* word to finish each sentence.

1. When she was still in the old country, Kate would _____ in bed and think about the long trip over here.

2. There was a chance that she would _____ on the long trip to the new country.

3. But she did not let these fears _____ her down to an unhappy life.

---

price
dice
nice
rice

A. Read the words in the box. Make other -*ice* words.

sl + ice = _____

tw + ice = _____

spl + ice = _____

B. Write an -*ice* word to finish each sentence.

1. Kate had to think _____ about going to a new land.

2. She loved the farm, but it would never make a _____ home for 11 people.

3. Losing the farm was the big _____ Kate paid for a new life.

Phonics: Long *i*

A. These letters can all stand for the long *i* sound: *ie, i-e, igh, i,* and *y.* Listen for the vowel sound in each word below. Underline the letters that stand for the long *i* sound.

ie	i-e	igh	i	y
die	rice	right	find	why
tie	five	high	child	try

B. Make other long *i* words. Read and write the words.

i-e

dr + ive = _____

l + ive = _____

thr + ive = _____

igh

br + ight = _____

fr + ight = _____

pl + ight = _____

i

m + ind = _____

w + ind = _____

bl + ind = _____

y

dr + y = _____

sk + y = _____

fl + y = _____

C. Write the vowel letters to make the words below.

1. Kate's grandmother cooked a lot of r_c_ to feed 11 people.

2. One of the smaller children did not m_nd Kate.

3. Kate had h____ hopes of making a new life in this country.

4. When there are 11 people in the family, you can't thr_v_ on a small farm.

Writing a Friendly Letter

A friendly letter is an informal letter, not a business letter. It can be typed or handwritten. Kate O'Dell still writes to her family back home. Her friendly letter might look like this.

[Month, day, year] June 18, 1987

[Opening]

Dear Jan,

    I've been telling Jean about the time on the ship with Nell, and the days I spent on Ellis Island. I can still see it all, after so many years.

[Main Part]

    I still think about the family, the old country, and our farm. Does it look the same?

    I hope you can come over here to see us before long. Jean would like to see you again, too. She was only a child the last time you were here. We'll have some good times together.

    I hope all is well with you.

Love,

Kate

[Closing]

A. Answer these questions about the letter.

1. When did Kate write the letter? _____

2. Other than the date, what is the first word of the letter? _____

3. What does Kate ask? _____

_____

4. How does the letter end? _____

B. Write a letter from Jan to Kate. What would Jan write back to Kate?

Going On

My grandmother has a light by her bed. You could not buy it from her, because she won't put a price on it. Kate likes to tell a story about it. Mike O'Dell gave the pretty light to Kate right after they met.

Mike O'Dell had been on Ellis Island, too. He came from Kate's country and had lived on a farm.

Mike was only 18 when he got here, but he was big for his age. When he got to the city, he found a job carrying bricks. At that time, many city streets were made of bricks, so Mike could always find work.

My grandmother found a job in a big home as a children's nurse. She tells us the story of how she took the children for their walk every day. And she well remembers the first time she saw Mike O'Dell. He was carrying heavy bricks along the street. He yelled at Kate to get out of the way.

How did Mike and Kate get together?

—Going On—

"I'll die before I take that kind of talk from a big lug like you!" Kate said to him. "Go off with your bricks and stop your yelling."

Mike listened to the way she talked. He could tell she was from the same part of the old country that he had come from. For the first time in a long time, he did not feel so lonely and foreign.

Kate and the children went to the park, so the children could play in the grass. Mike came over and sat down with them.

"You're a bold one!" said Kate, but she could not help laughing.

Kate and Mike talked about the old country and how homesick they were to see it again. They talked about trying to work farmland that couldn't give them good crops. Kate told Mike about her sister Nell.

Mike said, "I know what that feels like. My brother Will died on the way over, too."

The children got tired of playing and wanted to go home. Kate and Mike wanted to meet again. What a lucky thing it was that they both had their only day off on Sunday! They wanted to have a picnic in the country with good snacks to eat.

"I remember that first Sunday," my grandmother said. "Mike came up to me with this light in his hand and gave it to me. He must have paid a big price for it!"

"What did he say, Grandmother?" I asked.

"He told me that it wasn't good for me to think only of my old home and of the sad story of Nell," said Grandmother. "Mike wanted me to have the little light so that I would remember why I had come to this new country, and remember the good things I found here."

—Going On—

My grandmother winked at me. She said, "Mike O'Dell was one of the best people I found here. Before long I told him I wouldn't mind being Mrs. O'Dell, and he said he wouldn't mind having me for a wife. Your grandfather was a fine man, and we made a good life together."

The block where my grandmother lives became different as time went by. At first, only people like my grandparents lived there. Then people from different countries came to live on the same block.

My grandmother said, "At first, we had to get used to the new people. They had different names, different ways of talking, and different ways of doing things. Sometimes we would all fight, but little by little, we found out how to be friends."

"A lot of foreign people are moving to my block," I said, "but they didn't have to go to Ellis Island first."

"The island has not been used in that way for many, many years," said Grandmother. "There aren't many of us around who can remember the old days. We had to get used to different ways of doing things. At the same time, we always remembered and thought about the old country."

"Do you do that, Grandmother?" I asked. "Do you think a lot about that old farm by the water?"

Kate laughed. "Oh, only about once or twice a day," she said. "Most of the time I remember Mike O'Dell, and the fine family we had together."

She gave me a hug. "And you are one of the finest parts of that family," she said. "My story is part of your story, too, and when I die, I want you to have the little light for your own. It will help you to remember the story and tell it to your children and your grandchildren."

Comprehension: Sequence

Tips on Sequence

Sequence is about time. It means the order in which things happen. Use these hints to find the sequence of events in a story:

- Look for time words like *before, when, after, then, always, again, soon, still.*
- As you read, try to see the events as if they were part of a movie. Think about the beginning, what comes next, and the end.

A. Write 1, 2, and 3 to show the correct order of events.

_____ Nell died.

_____ Kate lived on a farm.

_____ Kate came to Ellis Island.

B. Underline the words that complete each sentence.

1. Kate worked as a nurse
   a. before she got on the ship.
   b. when she got to the city.
   c. after she had a family.

2. Kate and Mike first met
   a. when they were working.
   b. before they came to this country.
   c. after Kate had the light.

3. The little light
   a. will belong to Jean.
   b. belongs to Jean now.
   c. used to belong to Jean.

Life Skill: Reading a Map

river   library   north   south   east   west

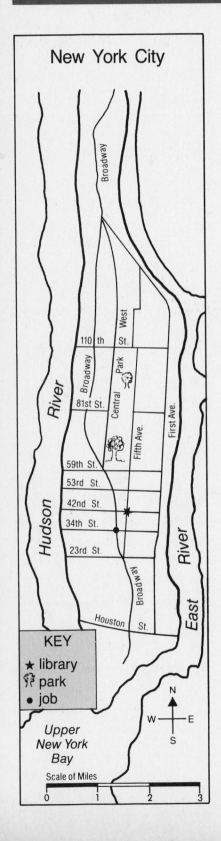

A. Read the new words. Then read the map.

B. Read the questions and write the answers.

1. If you got off a bus at 23rd Street and walked west, which river would you be headed for? _____

2. If you want to go to the library, where should you get off the bus? _____

   _____

3. After you go to the library, you want to find out about a job on 34th Street and Broadway. What are the two ways you can walk there? _____

   _____

   _____

4. If you were at 23rd Street and Broadway, would the park be north, south, east, or west? _____

Looking Out for Trouble

There go my two kids. The little one is so cute, and my older one is getting so big. They're going out to play in the park. The big child has his bat. He's nuts about baseball. Lan is tagging after him like she always does. Ming will look out for her; he's pretty responsible with his little sister.

I check on them from time to time. I go out and yell to them every now and then. They mind me—they don't give me a bad time like some people's kids do. People tell me, "Kim, your kids are so good."

Sometimes I don't like the kids I see around here. They don't live here, but they come around all the time. You can tell they're up to no good. They're looking for trouble, I always say. I tell Ming and Lan to come in right away if they think trouble is coming.

If I had my way, we wouldn't live here. We'd have a nicer home where my kids could play without problems. But, that's not how things are, so we try to make the best of it.

Review Words

A. Check the words you know.

- ☐ 1. kids
- ☐ 2. never
- ☐ 3. could
- ☐ 4. or
- ☐ 5. always
- ☐ 6. every
- ☐ 7. late
- ☐ 8. mean
- ☐ 9. party
- ☐ 10. club
- ☐ 11. once
- ☐ 12. around

B. Read and write these sentences.

1. Some mean kids live around here.

   _____

2. I never come home late from a party or movie.

   _____

   _____

3. A guard could check out every person who wants to come in.

   _____

   _____

C. Choose an answer from the words in the list.

1. a group you might be invited to join _____

2. all the time _____

3. one time _____

4. a fun event _____

5. not on time _____

6. children _____

7. not nice _____

Sight Words

show   project   safe   very

▶ I can <u>show</u> you that the <u>project</u> is not <u>very</u> <u>safe</u>.

A. Read the sight words above and the example sentence. Underline the sight words in 1—5.

1. The project that we live in is very big.

2. It isn't very safe for kids to play here.

3. I can show you where some people were mugged.

4. We asked the owners of the project to help us make it safe.

5. They were very nice but didn't show much interest in our problems.

B. Choose the words below to finish the sentences.

safe   show   project   very

1. We need more guards in this _____.

2. Most people don't feel very _____ here.

3. No one can come home _____ late.

4. We must _____ the problems to the owners.

C. Read the sentences. Underline the sight words.

A small child who lives in 10A had a very bad time this month. Some mean kids came into the project with a gun. It was a play gun, but little Zack didn't know that. The older kids showed the gun to him and made him let them in. They didn't take very much, but Zack was so upset. His family is new in the project, so he didn't know where to go to get help. Zack is OK now, but his mother is still very mad. She wants to work to make the project safe.

Sight Words

any   strangers   watch   grounds

▶ We want the guards to <u>watch</u> <u>any</u> <u>strangers</u> on the <u>grounds</u>.

A. Read the sight words above and the example sentence. Underline the sight words in 1—5.

1. We can't let any strangers come into the project.

2. Some of them make trouble on the grounds.

3. I tell my kids not to talk to any strangers.

4. We need a guard to watch the grounds.

5. A guard won't let strangers onto the grounds.

B. Choose the words below to finish the sentences.

any   grounds   watch   strangers

1. At first, the people who live together in a project are _____.

2. They need to _____ who tries to come in.

3. We can all use _____ help we can get.

4. We must guard the _____.

C. Read the sentences. Underline the sight words.

Some strangers are very friendly, but at our project we can't take any chances. I was coming home late one night after a party. I wasn't watching when some strangers came into the project grounds after me. I didn't know any of them and didn't know if they lived here. I found my key and went in. Then they came after me and hit me. I yelled for help. I was lucky that Mr. Price, the guard, was around. The men were arrested, and later, Mr. Price found out that they had prison records.

Sight Words

kind   town   worry   alone

▶ Ming is the <u>kind</u> of kid who likes going around <u>town</u> <u>alone</u>, and I <u>worry</u> about him.

A. Read the sight words above and the example sentence. Underline the sight words in 1–5.

1. This kind of project is like a small town.
2. Still, I worry when my kids go out alone.
3. I worry that I cannot watch them all the time.
4. Not all strangers will be kind to children.
5. Ming must learn to get around town alone.

B. Choose the words below to finish the sentences.

town   worry   alone   kind

1. Ming and Lan are the _____ of kids who don't stay home much.
2. Ming tells me not to _____ when he is out late at night.
3. Now that he's older, he thinks he can get around town _____.
4. I tell him that this is not always a friendly

_____.

C. Read the sentences. Underline the sight words.

I cannot keep my job and still be with my kids all the time. If we lived in a small town or in the country, maybe I could do it. But here, in this project in a big city, it's not safe for the kids to be alone. I worry because I've had problems and want to keep my kids from having the same kind of trouble.

Phonics: -ound and -own

---

grounds
around
found
rounds

A. Read the words in the box. Make other -ound words.

h + ound = _____

m + ound = _____

s + ound = _____

B. Write an -ound word to finish each sentence.

1. We need to put a gate _____ the grounds.
2. I feel safe at night when a guard is making his

   _____.

3. I called the guard when there was a strange

   _____ in the back room.

---

town
clown
crown
down

A. Read the words in the box. Make other -own words.

br + own = _____

dr + own = _____

fr + own = _____

B. Write an -own word to finish each sentence.

1. Our guard looks mean because of his _____,
   but he is a good guard.
2. We can tell who the guards are because they

   have _____ uniforms.

3. After the owners do what we've asked, this
   project will be one of the better ones in our

   _____.

Phonics: -*ou* and -*ow*

A. The letters *ou* and *ow* can stand for the same sound. Listen for the vowel sound in each word. Underline the letters that stand for the vowel sound.

1. found mound   2. town brown
   pound out   clown how

B. Make other words with *ou* and *ow*.

ou   *ow*

sh + out = _____   v + ow = _____

spr + out = _____   br + ow = _____

C. The letters *ou* can stand for more than one sound. Listen for the vowel sound in each word below. Underline the letters that stand for the vowel sound.

ou in **found**   *ou* in **you**
shout   mound   group   soup
pound   coupon

D. The letters *ow* can stand for more than one sound. Listen for the vowel sound in each word. Underline the letters that stand for the vowel sound.

ow in **down**   *ow* in **know**
how   frown   show   grow
brown   own

E. Write the vowel letters to make words below.

1. I don't want my kids to gr__ up in this project.

2. I've made a v__ to get them out of here.

3. Because I work two jobs, the children are on

   their __n much of the time.

Adding Endings to -y Words

try   tries   tried

Some action words end in y. Before adding an ending to these words, we change the y to i.

A. To write the new words, drop the letter y. Then add -ies or -ied.

	Add -ies	Add -ied
cry	_____	_____
spy	_____	_____
baby	_____	_____
worry	_____	_____
carry	_____	_____

B. Read the paragraph. Underline the words that end in -ies and -ied.

Lan cries when I tell her not to go out alone. Ming says that I have babied her too much. Time flies and she is getting older, but I still worry. Once, she couldn't find her way home. How I worried then! Now Lan belongs to a club and plays with kids her own age.

C. Choose the correct word below to finish each sentence.

cried   tries   carried   worries

1. Lan _____ not to talk to strangers.

2. Once, a woman in our project _____ for days because some people took all her furniture.

3. They _____ it off and no one stopped them.

4. Now she _____ that they will come back.

A Safe Home

What is Kim saying to this woman? What is the woman thinking?

Lan came home from school with some good tips today. She learned how to keep our home and family safe. She said all the kids went to a big meeting at school and talked about how to stay safe.

Some parents came to the meeting and told the kids this story: In April, their little son went out to play, and they couldn't find him for two days. The parents were sick with worry. They were so glad when they found their son. They wanted to help more children, so they told their story to the kids at Lan's school. Then a social worker gave every child a list of tips.

I've made up some tips of my own for parents. I'm going to take my list to a meeting here in the project. I hope we can work out better ways to keep our homes and children safe.

—Safe—

These are the tips I will talk about:

1. Tell your children not to talk to strangers in cars, in parks, or on the streets.
2. Know where your children are at all times. Teach them not to go out without telling you first. When they do go out, find out where they'll be.
3. Know who your children's friends are and where they live.
4. Don't let little children stay at home alone. Get someone to watch them.
5. Tell children of all ages not to let anyone in if you are not home.
6. Teach little children to remember their names and where they live.

• • •

The meeting at our project went very well. Most of the parents have been as worried as I have been. People who live alone are interested in helping, too. They think that if the project is safe for kids, it will be safe for everyone.

The project owners listened to us at this meeting. I think they could see by our plain talk that we will not be stopped. They can't afford to look away when we are working so hard. The day after the meeting, Ming and I went around to see every renter. We asked people to tell us how they would make the project safer.

—Safe—

A few days later, a group of renters met with the owners again and told them what we wanted. The owners said they would do some things to help us.

They're going to put more guards on the project grounds. The guards will stop all strangers and find out what they are doing or who they want to see. The guards will look out for the kids who live in the project too, and see that they don't clown around too much or get into trouble.

At night the gates around the grounds will be locked at nine. Only people who live here will have keys. A guard will stay in a small stand by the gate to check out the people who come and go.

City cops will work with our guards. They'll back up our guards by giving tickets, arresting troublemakers, and showing up when they are needed.

A list of tips for keeping children safe will be sent to all renters. Parents will be responsible for teaching their children to play it safe and to keep these tips in mind at all times.

We think that most people here in the project will be responsible and try to help. Parents, disabled people, older people, and children all have a lot to lose if we don't help each other.

Comprehension: Main Idea

Tips for Finding the Main Idea

The **main idea** is the point a writer or speaker is making about a subject. Use these tips to find the main idea:

- Read the whole paragraph or story.
- Decide what the whole story is about.
- Put the facts together to find the main idea.

A. Underline the correct answers.

1. The main idea of page 37 of the story is
   a. Lan went to an interesting meeting at school.
   b. Parents and children need to know tips about being safe.
   c. In April some parents couldn't find their child.

2. The main idea of the paragraphs on page 38 is
   a. People in the project are trying to work together.
   b. Ming is helping his mother talk to renters.
   c. People who live alone want to help.

3. The main idea of page 39 in the story is
   a. City cops will work with the project guards.
   b. The owners and renters are going to do many things to make the project safer.
   c. The gates will be locked at night.

B. Tell the main idea of this story in your own words.

_____

_____

Life Skill: Telephone Safety

telephone   number   emergency   address

A. Read the new words. Then read the tips that children should know when they answer the telephone.

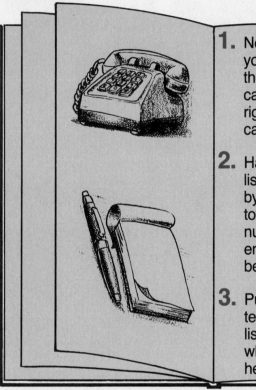

1. Never tell a stranger that you are home alone. Tell the caller that your parents can't come to the telephone right now. Ask for the caller's name and number.

2. Have your parents put a list of emergency numbers by the telephone. In many towns the emergency number is 911; or the emergency number may be 0.

3. Put your own address and telephone number on the list. This will help you when you are calling for help.

B. Read the questions and write the answers.

1. Your child is home alone. A stranger calls and asks to talk with you. Write what your child should say.

_____

_____

2. Why is it good to have your address and telephone number by the phone for a child to use in an emergency? _____

_____

_____

Clay's Best Friend

We all watch TV a lot in our family, but I think my son Clay has a problem with it. He likes TV too much. Clay plans his life around the TV. He needs to spend more time with his schoolwork. He did not get very good grades on his report card. It's like his life is TV. Clay tunes in to anything that's on, but the show he likes the best is *Back Streets*.

Back Streets is about two cops in a small town. Their names are Frank and Lucky. Frank is the bright one. He's always the first to find the person who did something wrong, and he's always the first one to make an arrest.

Lucky isn't so bright. Sometimes he can't find his own uniform. Sometimes he can't find his car! Most people who watch the show think Lucky is a lot of fun, but Clay doesn't think that way. He worries about Lucky and wants Lucky to do better work on the job.

Last month Clay said, "I feel bad about what Lucky is doing, Dad. People laugh at him. Frank is always putting him down. I'm going to tell Lucky how I feel."

"Oh, come on, Clay!" I said. "*Back Streets* is only a TV show. It's not life!"

"Yes it is!" said Clay. "I like Lucky, and I want him to know he has a friend out here."

Review Words

A. Check the words you know.

- ☐ 1. now
- ☐ 2. rules
- ☐ 3. lessons
- ☐ 4. grades
- ☐ 5. after
- ☐ 6. attendant
- ☐ 7. much
- ☐ 8. school
- ☐ 9. career
- ☐ 10. rock
- ☐ 11. know
- ☐ 12. report

B. Read and write these sentences.

1. I know that Clay likes to watch TV much more than he likes to do his lessons.

_____

_____

2. His report card from school shows that his grades are not very good.

_____

_____

3. After this, I'll have to make some new rules about Clay's schoolwork.

_____

_____

C. Choose an answer from the words in the list.

1. someone who helps do a job _____

2. some music is called _____

3. the work of a person's lifetime _____

4. at once _____

5. schoolwork _____

Sight Words

program	just	actor	those

▶ Those people on the program are just actors.

A. Read the sight words above and the example sentence. Underline the sight words in 1—5.

1. The man who plays Lucky on the program is a good actor.

2. Those programs can look just like life.

3. Dad watches the program with Clay just for laughs.

4. Clay doesn't remember that Lucky is just an actor.

5. Some of those TV programs upset Clay.

B. Choose the words below to finish the sentences.

those	programs	just	actors

1. *Back Streets* is one of the top _____ on TV.

2. The _____ get a lot of fame and money.

3. Clay doesn't think about _____ things.

4. He _____ worries about Lucky as if Lucky were a person.

C. Read the sentences. Underline the sight words.

Not all TV programs get to be in the top ten, but *Back Streets* is one of those programs that became a big hit right away. The men who play Frank and Lucky are very good actors. They are just like the cops around your own town. This program is very much like life. I just feel bad that Clay doesn't know that TV and life are different.

Sight Words

spoil   boy   real   hard

▶ I <u>spoil</u> things for my <u>boy</u> when I say that Lucky is played by <u>Rick</u> Reed, a <u>hard</u>-working actor in <u>real</u> life.

A. Read the sight words above and the example sentence. Underline the sight words in 1—4.

1. Rick Reed is a real person.

2. He became an actor when he was a boy.

3. In one movie part, his parents spoiled him.

4. He had a hard life and became a really bad man.

B. Choose the words below to finish the sentences.

real   boy   hard   spoil

1. I try to get Clay to work _____ on his lessons.

2. His _____ interest is the TV program.

3. My son is only a _____, but he needs to know that TV and real life are not the same.

4. "Don't talk now," says Clay. "When you talk, you

    _____ the TV program for me."

C. Read the sentences. Underline the sight words.

Maybe I'm wrong to hound Clay so much about what is real and what isn't. Maybe I spoiled the boy by letting him watch TV so much. I may have to make some rules for him about watching TV. "Do you think Rick Reed watches TV all day?" I asked Clay. "I bet he works hard and spends time with his friends."

"Who is Rick Reed?" Clay always asks.

Sight Words

study   letter   answer   mail

▶ Dad wants Clay to <u>study</u> hard, but Clay wants to <u>mail</u> a <u>letter</u> to Lucky and wait for an <u>answer</u>.

A. Read the sight words above and the example sentence. Underline the sight words in 1—5.

1. Clay sat down to write his letter to Lucky.

2. He said, "I'll write to Lucky, then I'll study hard."

3. "Do you think Lucky will answer your letter?" I asked.

4. "I know he'll answer my letter," said Clay.

5. Clay went down the street to mail the letter.

B. Choose the words below to finish the sentences.

studying   answer   letters   mail

1. Actors get fan _____ all the time.

2. Rick Reed reads many _____ every day.

3. Clay wants an _____ from Lucky, not from Rick Reed.

4. Clay is more interested in watching TV than

_____ .

C. Read the sentences. Underline the sight words.

Actors get a lot of fan mail. People write to them from all over the country. Rick Reed gets letters from lots of boys Clay's age. It must be hard for Rick Reed to answer so many letters. If Clay gets an answer, he may get interested in writing. Maybe he will study and won't watch TV so much.

Phonics: -*oil* and -*oy*

spoil

boil

soil

A. Read the words in the box. Make other -*oil* words.

c + oil = _____

f + oil = _____

t + oil = _____

br + oil = _____

B. Write an -*oil* word to finish each sentence.

1. Lucky makes so many mistakes on TV that he

may _____ Frank's plan to arrest people.

2. I think that I _____ Clay by letting him
watch TV before he does his homework.

3. Clay can make me so mad that I _____.

boy

coy

toy

A. Read the words in the box. Make other -oy words.

j + oy = _____

s + oy = _____

pl + oy = _____

B. Write an -oy word to finish each sentence.

1. It's strange that a TV show would give Clay so

much _____.

2. Clay is just a _____, but he should know
what is and isn't real.

3. It's only a _____ that Lucky lets Frank do
better than him on the show.

Phonics: -*oi* and -*oy*

A. The letters *oi* can be found at the beginning or middle of a word. Read each word below and circle the vowel letters *oi*.

oi-	*-oi-*	*-oi-*
oil	spoil	choice
oily	join	noise
ointment	point	hoist
	coin	poison

B. The letters *oy* can be found in the beginning, middle, or end of a word. Read each word below and circle the vowel letters *oy*.

oyster	joy	boycott
boy	annoy	employ
loyal	toy	disloyal
voyage	ahoy	joyful

C. Write the vowel letters to make words below.

1. Clay is a l__al fan of *Back Streets* and Lucky.

2. It really ann__s Clay when Lucky does everything wrong.

3. When I p__nt out that Lucky isn't a real person, Clay says I sp__l his fun of watching the program.

4. I don't want to make Clay stop watching *Back Streets,* but I may have no ch__ce.

Plural Possessive Nouns

brothers—brothers' room   **parents—parents' home**

To make most nouns plural, we add an s.
   One: brother   More than one: brothers

To make a noun show ownership, we add 's.
   brother   one *brother's* room

**To make a plural noun show ownership, we
add an apostrophe (') at the end of the word.**
   My two *brothers'* cars won't run.

**A. Change each noun to make it show ownership. Write
the plural possessive noun.**

1. players   the ten _____ chances

2. readers   four _____ books

3. guards   the _____ uniforms

4. doctors   three _____ clinics

**B. Decide if the noun shows one or more than one.
Then change the noun to make it show ownership.
Add 's or s'.**

1. parents   two _____ child

2. Nell   _____ sister

3. nurses   the _____ pins

4. actor   the _____ letter

**C. Read the paragraph. Underline the words that show
ownership.**

The fans' letters are fun for Rick to read. The
kids' thoughts are sometimes strange to him. They
don't know that an actor's job can be different from
year to year. Rick Reed would like to get some
parents' fan mail, too.

What's Real?

Why does Clay look like a cop?

May 1, 1987

Dear Lucky,
    I see you on "Back Streets" all the time.
People are always laughing at you because the
things you do are really strange. Why do you
let Frank get the better of you? In the last show,
you got sick from eating some spoiled food, and
you couldn't go out with Frank in the car. In
another show you just sat around acting like a
clown, so Frank went to work and arrested people.
    I think it's a shame that you don't do better
work as a cop. I always hope you'll show up Frank.
    I'm writing to you because I feel like a real
friend of yours. I hope you can clean up your act
so my family and friends will stop thinking you're
a dope.

Your friend,
Clay Brown

—Real—

June 30, 1987

Dear Clay,
     Thanks for your letter. It's good to know
that you watch "Back Streets." As an actor, I
like playing the part of Lucky. Lucky must be
very real to you, because you write to him as if
he were a real person. But remember that he's not
real. He's just a part I play on a TV show, and
I play the part to make people laugh.
     Someday, you may see me in another kind of
show. In my acting career, I've played many
different people. In one movie I was a mad doctor.
In another movie I was the star player in a rock
band. Just two months from now, I'll be playing
the part of an attendant in a clinic!
     Actors are always looking for different parts
to play. I've found some pretty good acting
projects, and the part of Lucky is just one of
them. I hope this letter hasn't spoiled "Back
Streets" for you!

                              Your friend,

                              Rick Reed

—Real—

I couldn't help feeling bad for Clay. He spent a long time reading Rick's letter over and over again.

"You see, Lucky isn't real," I said to Clay. "That's what Rick Reed is telling you in this letter. Lucky is just an actor's part in a hit TV program, but Rick Reed is real. He has an acting career, and he studies hard to get one good part after another in TV programs and movies."

"Lucky isn't going to be any different, is he?" asked Clay. "He's always going to be the one who people laugh at on *Back Streets*."

"That's right," I answered. "Rick Reed will go on to better and better parts. He's a fine actor."

Clay sat around thinking. It was time for *Back Streets*. "Don't you want to see the program?" I asked my boy.

"I don't think so," answered Clay. "I have some things to do right now, some real things." He went to his room.

•••

When the TV program was over, I went in to see Clay. What a shock I got! Clay had on a black hat, and he was hopping around and shouting.

"What's going on?" I asked.

"I'm going to be an actor," said Clay. "I'll have to work really hard at it. It will take a long time, but if Rick Reed can do it, so can I!"

So that's the way life is with my son Clay. Now he knows what's real and what's not real. But I don't know if I can stand an actor in my family!

Comprehension: Drawing Conclusions

Tips for Drawing Conclusions

A **conclusion** is a guess you make after thinking about all the facts you have. Use these tips to help you draw a conclusion:

- Read the whole paragraph or story.
- Study all the facts you read.
- Read between the lines. That is, decide what else the story is telling you.

A. Decide what conclusions you can draw from the story on pages 43 and 51—53. Underline the correct answers.

1. You can conclude that *Back Streets* is
   a. a program that is bad for children.
   b. the only program on TV.
   c. a program that many people like.

2. You can conclude that Rick Reed
   a. does not like to get letters.
   b. has a hard time finding jobs.
   c. likes to hear from his fans.

3. You can conclude that now Clay
   a. has a new interest to take the place of *Back Streets*.
   b. thinks actors are paid too much for their work.
   c. still thinks that Lucky is a real person.

B. Read your answers to Exercise A. Then read the parts of the story that helped you draw those conclusions.

Life Skill: Reading a TV Schedule

channel   rainbow   minute   hour

Monday
7:30 AM – 10 AM

7:35 (TBS) BEWITCHED—Comedy
7:45 (60) A.M. WEATHER
8 AM (4) ONE DAY AT A TIME—Comedy
(5) I LOVE LUCY—Comedy (BW)
(9) (18) (60) SESAME STREET (CC); 60 min.
(10) (13) POPEYE AND PALS—Cartoon
(35) SCOOBY DOO—Cartoon
(42) LEAVE IT TO BEAVER (BW)
(A&E) JAMES AT 16—Drama; 60 min.
(CBN) FLYING NUN—Comedy
(CNN) NEWS—Loughlin/Cain/Collins; 60 min.
8:05 (TBS) DOWN TO EARTH—Comedy
8:30 (4) PEOPLE'S COURT
(5) ALICE—Comedy
(10) (13) FLINTSTONES—Cartoon
(24C) CLASSIFIED VIDEO
(35) HEATHCLIFF—Cartoon
(42) (WGN) BEVERLY HILLBILLIES
(CBN) HAZEL—Comedy
(NSH) VIDEOCOUNTRY
(WOR) GIDGET—Comedy
8:35 (TBS) I LOVE LUCY—Comedy (BW)
9 AM (3) 3 MAGAZINE
(4) (5) PHIL DONAHUE; 60 min.
(4) (5) (7) (10) (13) $25,000 PYRAMID—Game
(6) LOVE BOAT—Comedy; 60 min.
(8) (23) (25) (36) FAMILY TIES
Part 1 of two. An expectant Elyse looks for-
ward to performing at Steven's TV station.
(9) (18) (60) MISTER ROGERS' NEIGHBOR-
HOOD—Children
9:30 (3) PEOPLE'S COURT
(4) (5) (7) (10) (13) NEW CARD SHARKS
—Game
(9) (18) (60) READING RAINBOW (CC)
(19) MONKEES—Comedy
(23) (25) (36) SALE OF THE CENTURY—Game
(24) PHIL DONAHUE; 60 min.
(35) I DREAM OF JEANNIE—Comedy
(42) BEWITCHED—Comedy
(NSH) FANDANGO—Game
(USA) GONG SHOW—Game

A. Read the new words. Then read the TV schedule.

B. Read the questions and write the answers.

1. Write the names of the game shows that are on TV at 9:30 A.M.

   _____

   _____

   _____

2. *Reading Rainbow* comes on at 9:30 A.M. What channels have this show?

   _____

3. a. When does the news show come on?

   _____

   b. How long is it? _____

   c. What is another way to say that?

   _____

   d. What channel is the news on?

   _____

4. *I Love Lucy* starts at 8 A.M. on channel 5.
   a. How long is this show?

   _____

   b. How can you tell? _____

   _____

A Home Away From Home

—June 14

It's hard to remember that I've only been here about a year. In some ways I feel that it's been longer. I feel so much at home here — the Prices are like my family. I like looking after their kids, Shelly and Ike, and helping to run their home. We all get along well together. The Prices are always saying, "What would we do without you, Pam?" And Mrs. Price's friend who lives down the street says, "I want someone just like you to help me when I have children."

But the letter I got today from my sister Rose made me feel homesick. She has always been my best friend as well as my sister, and I'm lonely when I think of her. It's hard to make friends in a new country. I don't meet many people because I work here in the Prices' home. Also, I'm shy about talking to strangers when I go out on my day off.

Sometimes I wish I could go home to see Rose, but I can't afford it. Anyway, I can't take that much time off because the Prices need me. How can they go to their jobs without someone to help out at home? I'll have to find another way ... maybe Rose could come to see me.

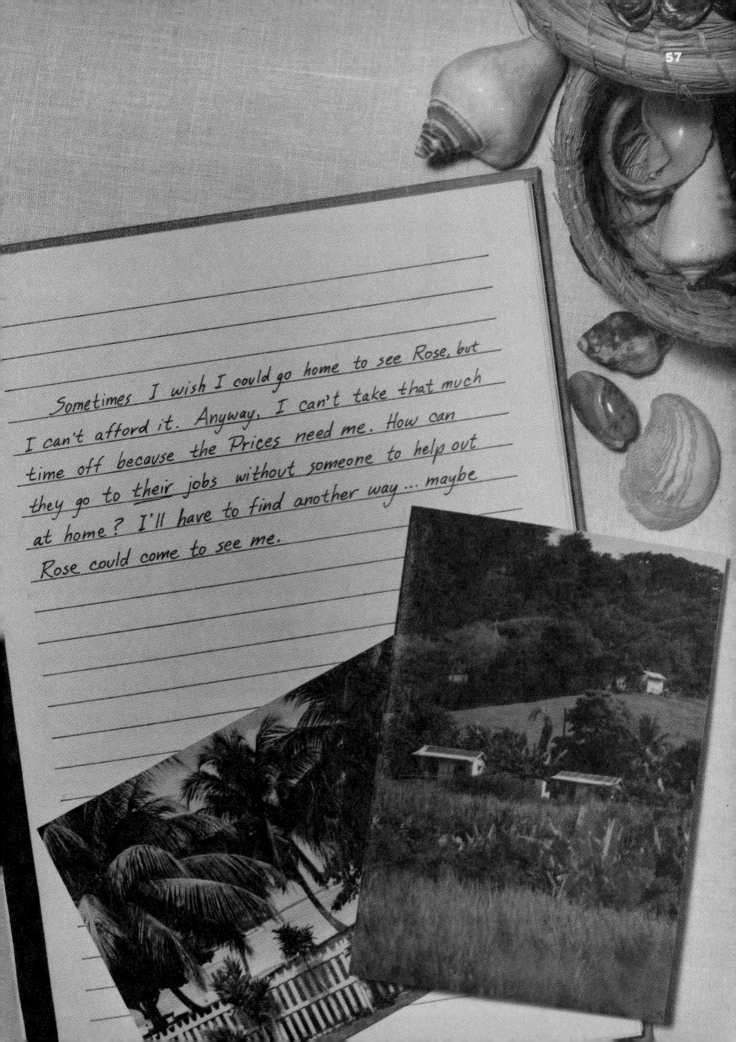

Review Words

A. Check the words you know.

- ☐ 1. picked
- ☐ 2. here
- ☐ 3. sweeping
- ☐ 4. if
- ☐ 5. been
- ☐ 6. before
- ☐ 7. cooking
- ☐ 8. then
- ☐ 9. sentence
- ☐ 10. year
- ☐ 11. blues
- ☐ 12. thinking

B. Read and write these sentences.

1. Pam stopped sweeping and cooking for a minute.

   _____

2. Then she picked up the card from Rose.

   _____

3. The last sentence said, "I've got the blues because I've been thinking of you." _____

   _____

   _____

4. Pam would be so glad if Rose could come to see her before this year is over. _____

   _____

C. Read the clues. Write the opposite of each clue in the puzzle.

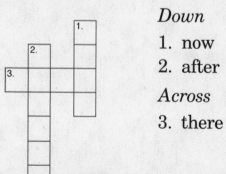

Down

1. now
2. after

Across

3. there

Sight Words

| permission | immigration | green | visit |

▶ Rose can <u>visit</u>, but she wants <u>permission</u> to work here.
<u>Immigration</u> laws say she must get a <u>green</u> card.

A. Read the sight words and the example sentences. Underline the sight words in 1—5.

1. I know about the immigration laws here.
2. It took me a long time to get my own green card.
3. Rose doesn't need permission to visit me.
4. If Rose wanted to work here, she would have to get a green card.
5. The immigration laws try to keep foreigners from taking work that people here could do.

B. Choose the words below to finish the sentences.

immigration   permission   visit   green

1. My island country is very _____ with lots of grass and trees.
2. I would like to go _____ my family.
3. There aren't many jobs on my island, so I got

    _____ to work here.
4. It's hard to meet the _____ laws.

C. Read the sentences. Underline the sight words.

When I first wanted to come to this country, I didn't know much about the immigration laws. I waited to get my green card so I would have permission to work for the Prices. Getting a green card is much harder than coming here to visit.

Sight Words

employer   house   goes   American

▶ My <u>American</u> <u>employer</u> <u>goes</u> out to work, and I work in the <u>house</u>.

A. Read the sight words and the example sentence. Underline the sight words in 1–4.

1. I keep house for my American employers.
2. I do the best I can with their house and the children.
3. The Prices gave me a responsible job and a small room in their house.
4. Some of the money I make goes to help my family back home.

B. Choose the words below to finish the sentences.

American   employers   goes   house

1. Some of my pay _____ to my family in the islands.
2. In many _____ families, both parents work.
3. These parents need someone to keep the _____ and babysit with the kids.
4. I was lucky to find nice _____.

C. Read the sentences. Underline the sight words.

The American immigration laws say I must have a green card to work in this country. Not many Americans want to be a housekeeper, so this kind of job goes to people like me. I'm lucky because the Prices are good employers.

Sight Words

papers   call   draw   legal

▶ I had to <u>call</u> on <u>legal</u> help to <u>draw</u> up the <u>papers</u> I needed for the immigration people.

A. Read the sight words and the example sentence. Underline the sight words in 1—4.

1. I needed legal help to get a green card.

2. Getting a green card takes time, money, and many calls, letters, and legal papers.

3. I had to draw money out of my savings to pay for the legal costs.

4. The immigration people checked to see that the legal papers were right.

B. Choose the words below to finish the sentences.

called   draw   legal   papers

1. The _____ costs for a green card are pretty high.

2. I never saw so many _____!

3. It takes a lot of time to _____ up so many papers.

4. I _____ many people for help.

C. Read the sentences. Underline the sight words.

Every day when Ike and Shelly come home from school, they call their mother at her job. Then they show me their drawings and school papers. We laugh and kid around. This draws my thoughts away from Rose and my island home. It's nice not to have legal papers to worry about anymore.

Phonics: -*all* and -*aw*

call

ball

fall

A. Read the words in the box. Make other -*all* words.

t + all = _____

w + all = _____

sm + all = _____

B. Write an -*all* word to finish each sentence.

1. I've spent hours trying to _____ the immigration people about my sister.

2. A _____ man with a kind look told me all the immigration rules.

3. When I met with them, they put me in a

_____ room with lots of other people.

draw

law

jaw

saw

A. Read the words in the box. Make other -*aw* words.

p + aw = _____

cl + aw = _____

fl + aw = _____

str + aw = _____

B. Write an -*aw* word to finish each sentence.

1. A person just can't know everything about

immigration _____.

2. I needed legal help to _____ up the papers.

3. They'll send the papers back to you if they find

a _____ in them.

Phonics: Syllables and Schwa

A. Listen for the number of word parts you hear in each word below. Each part is called a *syllable*, and each syllable has one vowel sound.

1 Syllable	2 Syllables	3 Syllables	4 Syllables
best	act-or	u-ni-form	A-mer-i-cans
spoil	af-ford	fur-ni-ture	Feb-ru-ar-y
threw	pro-gram	an-oth-er	im-mi-gra-tion

B. Listen for how many syllables you hear in each word below. Write the number.

parent _____   credit _____   responsible _____

foreigner _____   arrested _____   strain _____

C. Listen for the vowel sound in the underlined syllables below. This vowel sound is called the *schwa*. Each of the vowels—*a, e, i, o,* or *u*—can stand for the schwa sound.

a	e	i	o	u
a-lone	par-ent	fam-i-ly	pris-on	help-ful

D. Listen for the schwa sound in the words below. Write the letter that stands for the schwa sound.

about _____   sentence _____   doctor _____

April _____   actor _____   August _____

E. Choose a word from *A* to complete each sentence.

1. Most of my family live in _____ country.

2. They would like to come here and become

_____.

Irregular Verbs

drive—drove   **run—ran**

We add _-ed_ to some verbs to show the past. For other words, we change the spelling to show the past.

Example: I drive a car. (I am doing it _now_.)

I drove a car. (I did it _in the past_.)

A. Read this list of verbs.

Present	Past		Present	Past
keep	kept		write	wrote
draw	drew		know	knew
bring	brought		eat	ate
drive	drove		fight	fought
sweep	swept		swim	swam

B. Read the paragraph. Underline the verbs that show the past.

Rose wrote to Pam. Rose told about the legal work she was doing to get her green card. She brought her problems to a woman who drew up the papers she needed. Rose knew it would take a long time to get the green card. She fought hard not to get upset or give up trying.

C. Complete each sentence by choosing the verb that tells about the past.

1. Ike and Shelly _____ the food Pam cooked.
    ate   eat

2. Pam _____ and cleaned the house each
    sweep   swept
week.

3. When Pam lived in the islands, she _____
    swam   swim
in the water.

Hopes and Plans

—September 2

Rose came to visit, and we had the best time! She got along very well with the Prices, and they really liked her. They gave me as much time off work as they could, so Rose and I could be togther. I think they knew that I had been homesick for many months.

Shelly and Ike loved Rose, too. They were always giving her their drawings. The four of us played a lot of games in my room. How we laughed! I remember when Mrs. Price's friend, Mrs. Brown, came over. She came in to see what we were laughing about and pretty soon she was laughing, too. Now Rose is back in the islands and I'm lonely again.

—September 30

The mail came, and I got a letter from Rose today. She said that she had the best time on her visit. She said, too, that she really liked this country. Before her visit, she didn't think she would like it here. I wish she were here now.

—October 10

What good news! Mrs. Brown came over today to tell us that she's pregnant. But that's not all! Mrs. Brown wants Rose to work for her if Rose can get a green card. Then Rose can stay with the baby when Mrs. Brown goes back to work. I hope it works out!

—Hopes—

— October 18

Mrs. Price helped me write a letter to Rose. I told her about Mrs. Brown's baby and that she would like Rose to come and work for her. I told Rose that she would have to get a green card, like I did, and that it might take a long time. Writing that part made me remember how hard it is to get a green card.

— November 8

Mrs. Brown was here again. She is so cute when she talks about her baby. When the baby comes in June, Mrs. Brown will take six months off from work. I don't know ... I don't think Rose will have her green card by the time Mrs. Brown goes back to work. What will happen then? Will Mrs. Brown find another woman to look after the new baby?

— November 13

Rose wrote to me and to Mrs. Brown too. She wants very much to get her green card and come here to work. It may take two years, but it's something we can all work for.

— December 5

It's a good thing that Rose once had a housekeeping job in the islands because she must show the immigration people that she has housekeeping skills. Mrs. Brown must show that she ran ads and cannot find an American to do this job. I worry that she might find someone and then Rose won't get her green card.

—Hopes—

—June 17

The Browns now have a little boy! He is so cute. I'll write to Rose about him.

—July 30

I'm a little worried. Mrs. Brown says she likes being at home with the baby. What if she doesn't go back to work? What if she doesn't need Rose? Then my sister won't have a job.

— November 19

Mrs. Brown is going back to work in January, but Rose still doesn't have her green card. I don't know how this will end. I'm very worried.

— December 11

Mrs. Brown now plans to go back to work only part-time. She and Mr. Brown will plan their work schedules so that one of them will always be at home with the baby. This will be hard, but they're willing to wait for Rose to get her green card.

— September 24

Well, it's been a long year and a lot of hard work, but it's paying off. The immigration people say that Rose will be getting her green card soon. Just when, no one can say, but we hope it will be by the end of this year. What a party we'll have then! I don't know which one of us will feel luckier — Rose or Mrs. Brown or baby Tim or me.

Comprehension: Drawing Conclusions

Tips for Drawing Conclusions

A **conclusion** is a guess you make after thinking about all the facts you have. Use these tips to help you draw a conclusion:

- Read the whole sentence or paragraph.
- Study all the facts you read.
- Read between the lines. That is, decide what else the paragraph is telling you.

Decide what conclusions you can draw from the story on pages 56–57 and 65–67. Underline the correct answer.

1. You can conclude that Pam
   a. wants to find another job.
   b. likes it here and plans to stay.
   c. doesn't get along with her employer.

2. You can conclude that the Prices
   a. want to keep Pam as their housekeeper.
   b. work for the immigration people.
   c. want Rose to work for them.

3. You can conclude that a green card is
   a. for American workers.
   b. hard for foreigners to get.
   c. only for employers.

4. You can conclude that Mrs. Brown
   a. didn't think very highly of Pam.
   b. didn't remember what Rose was like.
   c. thought Rose would be a good worker.

Life Skill: Filling Out a Form

middle　　　form　　　information　　　male　　　female

A. Read the new words. Then read the form below. A person who is trying to get a green card might fill out a form like this.

U.S. Department of Justice	FORM G-325A	OMB No. 1115-0066
Immigration and Naturalization Service	BIOGRAPHIC INFORMATION	

1. (Family name) (First name) (Middle name) | ☐ MALE ☐ FEMALE | BIRTHDATE(Mo.-Day-Yr.) | NATIONALITY | FILE NUMBER A

2. ALL OTHER NAMES USED (Including names by previous marriages) | CITY AND COUNTRY OF BIRTH | SOCIAL SECURITY NO. (If any)

3. FAMILY NAME　FIRST NAME　DATE, CITY AND COUNTRY OF BIRTH(If known)　CITY AND COUNTRY OF RESIDENCE.
FATHER
MOTHER(Maiden name)

4. HUSBAND(If none, so state) OR WIFE　FAMILY NAME (For wife, give maiden name)　FIRST NAME　BIRTHDATE　CITY & COUNTRY OF BIRTH　DATE OF MARRIAGE　PLACE OF MARRIAGE

5. FORMER HUSBANDS OR WIVES(if none, so state)
FAMILY NAME (For wife, give maiden name)　FIRST NAME　BIRTHDATE　DATE & PLACE OF MARRIAGE　DATE AND PLACE OF TERMINATION OF MARRIAGE

6. APPLICANT'S RESIDENCE LAST FIVE YEARS. LIST PRESENT ADDRESS FIRST.

STREET AND NUMBER	CITY	PROVINCE OR STATE	COUNTRY	FROM MONTH	YEAR	TO MONTH	YEAR
						PRESENT TIME	

B. Read the questions and write the answers.

1. Would Rose write the word Rose as her family name, first name, or middle name on the form?

_____

2. On which line would Pam give information about her parents? _____

3. Would Pam check male or female on the form?

_____

4. On which line of the form would Pam give information about where she lives? _____

He Saw Her!

Pedro stopped at the card shop on his way home from work. He still had his work uniform on and it wasn't very clean, but he planned to get in and out of the shop before anyone saw him. He just needed a get-well card for a friend. If he got the card now, he wouldn't have to worry about it again.

There were lots of people in the shop, but Pedro had no trouble slipping to the back. The real problem was picking a card to buy. Pedro couldn't make up his mind. He was just about to pick a big green one when something made him look up. It wasn't something; it was someone—the best-looking someone in all the city. Pedro forgot what he had been doing. He could only stand there looking at her.

"Could I get by you?" a man asked. "I'd like to look at those cards."

Pedro let the man go by. Then he walked around the shop. He just had to find out who she was. What was her name? Did she work here? How could he get to know her? She was walking around the store looking at the cards. Pedro picked up the green card again and went to pay for it. He hoped she would come over to take his money, but he wasn't so lucky.

Review Words

A. Check the words you know.

- [ ] 1. saw
- [ ] 2. must
- [ ] 3. summer
- [ ] 4. how
- [ ] 5. soon
- [ ] 6. thank
- [ ] 7. too
- [ ] 8. ask
- [ ] 9. would
- [ ] 10. why
- [ ] 11. card
- [ ] 12. better

B. Read and write these sentences.

1. Pedro saw someone at the card shop who he would like to know better.

_____

_____

2. How would he talk to someone who was so pretty?

_____

_____

3. Why was he too shy to ask her for a date?

_____

_____

C. Read the clues. Complete the puzzle.

Across

1. the part of the year that comes after spring
3. Tell someone you are glad for the help.

Down

1. right away
2. need to or have to

Sight Words

girl noticed true start

▶ Pedro <u>noticed</u> the <u>girl</u> right from the <u>start</u>.
"I <u>think</u> I've found my <u>true</u> love!" he said.

A. **Read the sight words above and the example sentences. Underline the sight words in 1—5.**

1. Pedro noticed the girl right away.

2. Seeing her for the first time gave him a start.

3. She was too good to be true!

4. Pedro didn't know if the girl noticed him.

5. He wanted to say something but didn't know where to start.

B. **Choose the words below to finish the sentences.**

girl true started notice

1. Pedro _____ to pay for his card.

2. He hoped to meet the _____.

3. Would she _____ him standing there?

4. Was it _____ that she worked in the card shop?

C. **Read the sentences. Underline the sight words.**

Pedro couldn't get the girl from the card shop out of his mind. He started thinking about how he could meet her. He would go back to the shop and get her to notice him. It was true that he didn't need more cards, but he would go back anyway.

Sight Words

idea   few   open   birthday

▶ Pedro's idea was to look for a <u>few</u> <u>birthday</u> cards if the shop was <u>open</u>.

A. Read the sight words above and the example sentence. Underline the sight words in 1—4.

1. Pedro's idea was to go back to the shop soon.

2. He would look at the birthday cards this time.

3. The shop was open, but only a few people were there.

4. Pedro had no idea what to say to the girl.

B. Choose the words below to finish the sentences.

birthday   open   few   ideas

1. Pedro looked at a _____ different cards.

2. Some of the _____ in them were pretty good.

3. Pedro did not know anyone who was having a

   _____ soon.

4. Pedro saw the girl _____ a card and show it to a customer.

C. Read the sentences. Underline the sight words.

Pedro opened one card after another. Soon he would have to buy a few. The girl would get the wrong idea if he didn't buy some, so he picked out a few birthday cards and went to her. When he tried to pay her, he dropped his money. The girl didn't say anything, but Pedro got the idea that she must be laughing at him.

Sight Words

please	wish	warm	far

▶ Pedro's <u>wish</u> was to <u>please</u> the girl, but he didn't get very <u>far</u>. Her look was not <u>warm</u>.

A. Read the sight words above and the example sentences. Underline the sight words in 1—4.

1. Pedro wished to talk to the girl, but he was shy.
2. "Please tell me your name," he asked.
3. He learned that her name was Ana, but still he was far from asking her out.
4. "Please tell me why you buy so many cards," she said.
5. Pedro started to feel warm all over and forgot what he wanted to say.

B. Choose the words below to finish the sentences.

warmly	pleased	far	wished

1. Pedro _____ that he could tell Ana the real story.

2. He hoped that she would act _____ to him.

3. Would she be _____ that he liked her?

4. How _____ would he go to get Ana interested in him?

C. Read the sentences. Underline the sight words.

Pedro wasn't too pleased about buying so many cards. "I wish I could think of another way to see Ana," he thought. "She doesn't know me, so I won't get too far if I just ask her out. I wish I could get her to warm up to the idea of a date."

Phonics: -ue and -ew

true

blue

due

A. Read the words in the box. Make more -ue words.

cl + ue = _____

fl + ue = _____

gl + ue = _____

B. Write an -ue word to finish each sentence.

1. It's _____ that Pedro wanted Ana to notice him.

2. He picked out a _____ and green birthday card in the shop.

3. He has many other cards, but he hasn't a _____ about what they say.

few

grew

chew

new

A. Read the words in the box. Make more -ew words.

bl + ew = _____

cr + ew = _____

thr + ew = _____

B. Write an -ew word to finish each sentence.

1. Pedro _____ very shy when Ana looked at him.

2. He went back to the shop and got a _____ more cards.

3. He _____ out many cards that he would never use.

Phonics: o͞o and o͝o

A. **The letters o͞o can stand for the long vowel sound heard in *food*. The letters *ue*, *ew*, and *ou* can stand for the same sound. Underline the vowels below.**

o͞o	ue	ew	ou
food	blue	blew	group
mood	clue	chew	soup

B. **Make other words with o͞o.**

m + oon = _____   c + ool = _____

n + oon = _____   p + ool = _____

sw + oon = _____   st + ool = _____

C. **The letters o͝o can stand for the short vowel sound heard in *good*. The letters *ou* can also stand for this sound. Underline the vowels below.**

o͝o		ou	
good	hood	could	should
wood	stood	would	

D. **Make other words with o͝o below.**

b + ook = _____   br + ook = _____

c + ook = _____   cr + ook = _____

h + ook = _____   sh + ook = _____

E. **Choose a word from above to complete each sentence.**

1. Pedro tried to be _____ when he talked to Ana, but he grew warm.

2. Pedro was so shy around Ana that his hand

_____

Reflexive Pronouns

my + self = myself   **them + selves = themselves**

A. **Add the word *self* to the words you already know to make the new words.**

Add *-self*

him   _____

her   _____

your   _____

B. **The plural of *self* is *selves*. Add *selves* to these words.**

Add *-selves*

your   _____

them   _____

our   _____

C. **Complete the sentence by choosing the correct pronoun.**

1. "Can you put out all those cards by

   _____, or do you need some help?"
   　　yourself　　himself
   Ana's employer asked her.

2. Ana and her helper could do the work

   _____, so their boss went to see a
   　　themselves　　myself
   customer.

3. "We can do this _____ in about
   　　　　　　myself　　ourselves
   an hour," Ana told her helper.

Will They Meet?

Pedro sat in his room talking to himself about Ana. Just going into the shop and buying cards wasn't doing him much good. Ana noticed that he had picked out a lot of birthday cards, but she didn't notice him. To Ana, he was only a customer who came into the shop.

"She must have a boyfriend," Pedro said to himself. He didn't like to think about that problem.

"Could I call her?" he asked himself. "No! She doesn't know my name."

"Will it do any good to buy more cards?" he thought. "No! She just tells me the price and takes my money. I can't afford to spend all my money on cards!"

Pedro picked up a card with blue, green, and red stars. "Cute," said Pedro, "but what will I do with it?"

How does Pedro get to know Ana better?

—Meet—

Then Pedro got his bright idea. At first he liked the idea. "Why not?" he asked himself. Then he didn't like it. "Who am I kidding?" he said. Then he liked it again. "I'll try it!" he cried. "After all, what can I lose?"

So Pedro got a pen and sat down at his table. He opened the card and started to write.

After work on Monday, Pedro went back to the card shop once more. This time he didn't buy anything. He went straight to where Ana was working and saw she was alone. Good! He didn't want to get Ana in trouble with her boss. Pedro gave her the card.

"It's for you," he said. "I picked it out myself."

Ana looked up. "For me?" she asked. "Why?" She started to open the card. Pedro grew worried. What was she going to think?

Ana looked at the card, then at Pedro. "Thanks," she said, "but why are you giving me a card?"

Pedro looked down at the ground. "Well, I just wanted to thank you for being so nice to me," he said.

Ana laughed warmly. "But why are you giving a card to someone you don't know? I thought you sent all those cards to your friends in faraway towns."

Pedro didn't know what to answer, but he had to come up with something. After all, she was talking to him. He grew warm at the thought. She *was* talking to him!

"I do, but I like to have friends here, too," he said.

Ana grinned. "That's very nice," she said. "It's a little strange, but nice." After a few minutes she said, "It's no fun to sell cards if you don't get any."

Pedro was pleased. This was a good start!

—Meet—

"Now I know your name," said Ana, "because it's on the card. I didn't know how to find out who you are. You always get so red when I look at you. Pedro is a nice name. I like it."

Pedro got very red.

"Listen," Ana went on, "if we're going to be friends, we need to know more about one another. I get off work soon. Can you stay around?"

Pedro grinned. "You bet!" he said. "I'll just look at the cards."

Ana winked at him and said, "Don't tell me you need more cards. You must have cards all over your house."

Pedro laughed at that. "It's true! I could open a card store myself, but then I wouldn't get to see you," he said boldly. He didn't feel so shy anymore. Ana was fun to talk to, and she was very open.

Pedro went around to a small card rack that he had noticed a few days before. He had lots of birthday cards and holiday cards, but there was one kind of card he didn't have. He looked for just the right one. This one? No, that was too plain. That one? Then Pedro saw the card he wanted. "That will do very well," he thought. "I hope I'll need it soon."

Pedro slipped the card in a bag so Ana wouldn't see it. He didn't want her to see it just yet, so he told her how much it cost and paid for it. He waited while Ana locked up the card shop.

Then he and Ana walked over to a snack shop where they sat together at a small table and talked for a long time. Pedro's newest card, the one that said "I love you," was in the bag on the table. Some day, not yet, he might give it to Ana.

Comprehension: Using Context

Tips for Using Context

Using **context** means learning a new word by looking at all the other words in a sentence or paragraph. When you use context, you decide which meaning for the word you are learning best fits with the other words in the sentence.

A. Use context to figure out the meaning of the word in color.

Ana was a **clerk** in a card shop.

- Could *clerk* mean *customer*? _____ (Clue: Ana does not buy any cards.)

- Could it mean *owner*? _____ (Clue: We know Ana has a boss.)

- Could it mean a *worker* who helps the customers?

_____ (That does make sense.)

B. The paragraph below has two words in color. Use context to decide what the words mean.

Pedro wants to ask Ana to go out with him. He fears that if he asks her, she will say no. He is **afraid** to ask her out on a date. If she **rejects** him, he will be very sad.

1. To be **afraid** means to _____.

   fear   want   like

2. To **reject** means to _____.

   say yes   help   say no

Life Skill: Reading a Menu

menu   extras   least   beverages

A. Read the new words. Then read the menu below.

EATS
C A F E

BAR-B-QUE
SERVED WITH CHOICE OF TWO EXTRAS

Pork Ribs	$ 7.95
Brisket	$ 7.50
Sausage	$ 5.95
Chicken	$ 6.50
Combo	$10.50

(Brisket, Ribs, Sausage)

GOOD EATS
SERVED WITH CHOICE OF TWO EXTRAS

Chicken Fried Steak	$6.50
Chicken Fried Chicken	$6.95

VEGGIE PLATE
Choice of three extras .. $4.95
and cornbread

DINNER SALAD
Blue Cheese, Creamy Herb
or Ranch $1.50

DESSERTS
Ask For Today's Selection

GRILL
SERVED WITH CHOICE OF TWO EXTRAS

Shrimp	$10.95
Filet Mignon	$ 7.95
Sirloin	$ 7.75
Chopped Steak	$ 5.25
Grilled Chicken	$ 6.50

SANDWICHES
WHITE OR WHOLE WHEAT
SERVED WITH ONE EXTRA

Brisket	$4.25
Sausage	$3.95
Chopped Beef	$3.95
Hamburger	$4.50
Cheeseburger	$4.75
Chicken, Avocado, Provolone	$5.25

BEVERAGES

Coke	$.95
Diet Coke	$.95
Dr. Pepper	$.95
Sprite	$.95

EXTRAS . . . . . $1.50 each

Beans	Onion Rings	Blackeyed Peas
Dirty Rice	Mashed Potatoes	Broccoli
Potato Salad		Squash

B. Read the questions and write the answers.

1. a. What foods on the menu cost the least, other than the beverages? _____

    _____

    b. What food costs the most? _____

2. If you want a cold drink, what heading should you look under? _____

3. If you want to eat sausage but only have $5, what will you pick? _____

A Block About To Die

Pablo could never walk home from work at night without feeling some shame about the way his block looked. This part of town was going downhill fast. House after house and wall after wall was full of writing and stains. Kids liked to write their names or draw all over the walls, and the drawings were not good. It isn't legal to do this kind of thing, but the cops have a really hard time keeping up with the problem.

Pablo's roommate Martino walked up to him. "Look at all this!" said Pablo. "A stranger coming here would think we don't know any better. This block is really a sad sight!"

"I feel the same way you do," said Martino. "I worry about the problem, but I don't know how to stop the kids who are responsible."

When Pablo came to his mother's house, he saw his mother and his grandmother outside. His grandmother was yelling. "Look at those big green letters all over the side of our house!" she said. "Your mother and I noticed them here today when we got home from the store. I could have died when I found them!"

"This is it!" said Pablo. "Now these kids have spoiled my family's house! They went too far this time. I'll show them! Those kids will pay for this!"

"Don't get mad," said Martino. "You and I can find a way to cope with this problem without starting a fight with people on our block."

Review Words

A. Check the words you know.

- ☐ 1. put
- ☐ 2. small
- ☐ 3. roommate
- ☐ 4. as
- ☐ 5. tired
- ☐ 6. listen
- ☐ 7. now
- ☐ 8. again
- ☐ 9. responsible
- ☐ 10. join
- ☐ 11. yours
- ☐ 12. where

B. Read and write these sentences.

1. Pablo and his roommate are tired of this block.

   _____

2. Where can they go now to see a clean block?

   _____

   _____

3. They will have to put up with the problem as long as those kids will not be responsible.

   _____

   _____

C. Match the word with the definition.

1. yours

2. again

3. listen

4. small

5. join

When you put parts together, you ══ them.

When I talk to you, please ══.

When something belongs to you, it is ══.

When you do something over, you do it ══.

If something is not big, it may be ══.

Sight Words

born neighborhood building fast

▶ Pablo was <u>born</u> in a <u>building</u> in this <u>neighborhood</u>, and he saw the city grow <u>fast</u>.

A. Read the sight words above and the example sentence. Underline the sight words in 1—3.

1. Pablo's family still lives in the building where he was born.

2. His mother and father were born in another country, and grew up there.

3. They don't like to see the buildings in their neighborhood grow old so fast.

B. Choose the words below to finish the sentences.

born   neighborhood   buildings   fast

1. At the time Pablo was _____, this building still looked pretty good.

2. Some years back, it was fun to live in a building in this _____.

3. Now some kids are working _____ to make the block look bad.

4. Lots of people would like the _____ in the neighborhood to look good again.

C. Read the sentences. Underline the sight words.

"We can't afford to let these buildings get run down," Pablo thinks to himself. "Martino and I have to do something fast. I'm a born fighter, so I get madder and madder when I see what some people do to the buildings in this neighborhood."

Sight Words

marks	full	done	paint

▶ The buildings are <u>full</u> of <u>marks</u> <u>done</u> with <u>paint</u>.

A. Read the sight words above and the example sentence. Underline the sight words in 1—4.

1. Martino and Pablo talked to their employer about the paint marks.
2. Mrs. Chapa said, "Yes, the neighborhood is full of that kind of thing."
3. "Little by little, it's being done all over the city."
4. "Kids want to stand out in some way, so they do it by marking buildings with their names."

B. Choose the words below to finish the sentences.

mark	full	done	paint

1. A few kids have some _____ in spray cans.
2. They _____ up any big wall they find.
3. When a wall is _____, they do another one.
4. What they have _____ makes other people very mad.

C. Read the sentences. Underline the sight words.

"If only I could get my hands on the kids who have done this!" Pablo says to himself. "It's the same kids, again and again. Our block is full of the marks they have made. They think that they can paint any wall they see. Their marked-up walls spoil the neighborhood for everyone. If we get the paint off, a few days later the wall is marked up again. We are tired of looking at their paint jobs."

Sight Words

under   art   creative   color

▶ I studied <u>art</u> and <u>color</u> <u>under</u> a <u>creative</u> teacher.

A. Read the sight words above and the example sentence. Underline the sight words in 1—5.

1. "Art was my big interest as a kid," said Pablo.
2. Martino said, "I liked art and color, too."
3. "I write my name under my best drawings," Martino said.
4. Pablo said, "I bet these kids with spray cans could be more creative with color."
5. "If we do some creative thinking, we can find a way to help them," said Mrs. Chapa.

B. Choose the words below to finish the sentences.

art   color   under   creative

1. _____ all these paint marks is a plain wall.
2. We need works of _____ on buildings.
3. Most buildings around here could use some _____ if it were put on the right way.
4. _____ kids could make the block look good.

C. Read the sentences. Underline the sight words.

Pablo, Martino, and Mrs. Chapa talked about starting an art project. They needed to talk to the kids who were marking up the buildings with paint, and teach them to be more creative with color. "To get this project under way," Mrs. Chapa said, "I'll pay for the paint."

Phonics: -*ark* and -*orn*

---

mark
bark
dark
lark

A. Read the words in the box. Make other -*ark* words.

p + ark = _____

sh + ark = _____

sp + ark = _____

B. Write an -*ark* word to finish each sentence.

1. Those kids like to _____ on the walls of our block.

2. They paint the walls after _____ so we won't see them.

3. Pablo won't _____ his car on this block now because the kids could paint it.

---

born
corn
horn
torn
worn

A. Read the words in the box. Make other -*orn* words.

sc + orn = _____

sw + orn = _____

th + orn = _____

B. Write an -*orn* word to finish each sentence.

1. The paint looks _____ on some walls, so we try to clean them.

2. This is not like the city where I was _____. People there didn't write on walls.

3. Most people _____ this kind of act that makes their block look run down.

Phonics: Vowels With *r*

A. Vowels followed by *r* sound different. Listen to the vowel sound in each word below. Underline the two letters that stand for the first vowel sound.

ar	ir	or	er	ur
hard	girl	born	her	nurse
art	birthday	fork	person	Thursday

B. Make other words that have vowels with *r*. Read and write the words.

-ar

c + art = _____

st + art = _____

ch + art = _____

-ir

sw + irl = _____

tw + irl = _____

wh + irl = _____

-or

c + ork = _____

p + ork = _____

Y + ork = _____

-ur

c + urse = _____

n + urse = _____

p + urse = _____

C. Write the letters to make the words below.

1. Pablo and Martino want to st__t an art project for the block.

2. They want to stop the c__se of the spray paint that spoils the look of their block.

3. Pablo used to live in the big city of New Y__k.

Adding -es to Words

watch—watches   **wish—wishes**

Sometimes we add -es instead of -s to nouns to show more than one. Some verbs also end in -es.

A. Read the words. Add -es to make the new word.

Add *-es* to Nouns	Add *-es* to Verbs
1. bus _____	1. teach _____
2. grass _____	2. fix _____
3. boss _____	3. wish _____
4. box _____	4. watch _____

B. Read the paragraph. Underline the words that end in -es.

Mrs. Chapa buys some boxes of paint for the art project. She wishes other people would give her more things the kids will need. Pablo teaches the smaller boys to paint, but Mrs. Chapa teaches Pablo how to run a neighborhood project. She watches Pablo talk to the kids and gives him more ideas.

C. Write the word that completes each sentence.

fixes   wishes   buses

1. Pablo _____ that the neighborhood looked better.

2. The _____ and buildings are marked up with paint.

3. This art project really _____ up the neighborhood.

The Painting Project

One night, Martino and Pablo went around and talked to the kids who were spoiling the buildings.

Martino said, "You kids like putting paint all over walls. We want you to put that interest into something more creative. Put real art on the walls."

"What are you trying to pull on us?" the boy named Roberto asked. "We don't know about art!"

"That's what you think!" Pablo answered. "You've been painting and drawing all this time. If you join our program, you can keep on doing all that, but now you can make the buildings look nice, not spoiled and worn out. You can still show off your skill, but you can do it in a way that will make people in the neighborhood feel good about you."

*Who painted this?
Why?*

—Painting—

Another kid, Benito, said, "It doesn't sound like much fun."

"Look," Pablo said, as he took out a drawing. "I made this myself. This drawing shows the life story of my family. It shows how my parents came to America, and it shows my sister and me as little kids."

"So what?" asked Roberto. "So you made a little drawing. We like to do things big!"

"I could take this same drawing and do it really big on the side of a building," Pablo said. "Then I could paint in the colors. I couldn't do it fast, but I could do it well. The painting would stand out, and it would make an old building look good."

Roberto, Benito, and their friends looked at Pablo's drawing. They began to get some creative ideas of their own. Roberto said, "I have a story that's more interesting. It's about the time my brother was put under arrest, went to prison, and then got out. My family found him a good job. I could paint that."

All the kids had a story to tell. Martino and Pablo just listened. They got the feeling that they had sparked an interest in the art program.

Roberto said, "What if we go along with this art project? Where will we get the paint? You need good paint to make good art, and we can't afford it."

"Our boss, Mrs. Chapa, says she's willing to pay for the paint," Pablo said. "I can talk to other people who own stores around here. They'll give us money to buy what we need. People here will back you up when you do something that helps the neighborhood."

—Painting—

The boys looked at one another. "OK," said Roberto. "We'll give it a try. I'm sick of working in the dark anyway. Now we can mark up buildings in the daylight!"

• • •

Pablo wished that people all over the country could see the block after the kids had been very creative. They had put a lot of time into their paintings. The neighborhood people had good feelings about the boys who did the paintings.

One Saturday, Roberto came over and talked to Pablo. He said, "Every wall on every building around here is filled with art now. I wish there were some more creative work we could do."

"You can keep this program going," Pablo said. "Have you looked hard at some of the other blocks in this city? They look run down and marked up, just like this block did once. Why don't you talk to some of the kids on those blocks? Get them interested in a creative art project like this one."

Roberto looked at Pablo. "Are you telling me that you want me to be an art boss?" he asked. "I could have sworn that I would never be the boss of anything!"

"You don't have to be a boss, Roberto," Pablo laughed. "You just have to help kids learn to do their very best. Show them what you and your friends have done. I bet other kids will have creative ideas."

Pablo looked around at all the buildings. They were full of color and life. "You know, Roberto," he said, "I get a warm feeling when I come home to this block."

"So do I," said Roberto.

Comprehension: Using Context

Tips for Using Context

Using **context** means learning a new word by looking at all the other words in a sentence or paragraph. When you use context, you decide which meaning for the new word best fits with the other words. Here are some tips for using context:

- Read the sentence to the end; don't stop at the new word.
- Ask yourself what word would make sense.
- See if that meaning fits in the sentence.

Think about the story in this unit. Read each sentence below. Study the words in color. Then underline the word choice that best fits with the sentence and tells what the new word means.

1. I **recall** being a child on this block.
   a. ask about   b. remember   c. worry about

2. After all this time, I **continue** to live here.
   a. no longer   b. hate   c. still

3. I must **protect** my home from kids who want to spoil it.
   a. guard   b. project   c. clean

4. Some bad kids are trying to **ruin** the buildings on the block.
   a. spoil   b. rain   c. save

5. I **discovered** who these troublemakers were.
   a. drew   b. lied about   c. found out

Life Skill: Reading Help Wanted Ads

experienced   references   apartments

#	Ad
1	NEEDED: Experienced Route Salesperson. 836-6127
2	NOW ACCEPTING Applications for teachers. La Petit Acadamy, Brodie Lane. 282-9789.
3	OWNER OPERATORS for city delivery wanted. Good driving record and good equipment needed. Send resumes to 3805 Woodbury. Do not apply in person.
4	PAINTER/MAKE Ready needed at Harper's Creek Apartments at 1730 East Oltorf. Experienced only. Must have references.
5	PART TIME, Full time opportunity in marketing. Hours flexible. Call Thursday. 469-9000 ext. 2328 for interview.
6	PART TIME grounds keeper needed at apartment complex located North Central. Must maintain grounds and pools. Compensation is apartment only. 451-4561, 442-4076.
7	FULL AND Part Time Cashiers Needed. Apply in person only at Texaco 7510 First Street.
8	FULL TIME Cashier—Monday-Saturday. Must have sewing experience. Call for appointment. Gem Fabrics, 452-5024.
9	GENERAL PART TIME office help. Must have pleasant phone voice. Minimal typing. Interviews on Monday, Tuesday, 8/11, 8/12, 9am-1pm. Call for appointment: 282-7414.
10	GOLD MINE FULL TIME MANAGER APPLY AT NORTHCROSS MALL
11	GROUNDSKEEPER/PAINTER— Needed full time. Anderson Oaks Apartments. 9219 Anderson Mill Road.
12	GYMNASIUM INSTRUCTORS FOR FALL CLASSES 282-7739
13	HELP WANTED at full service station. Mechanical knowledge helpful but not necessary. Come by 2715 Hancock Dr.
14	HOUSEKEEPER NEEDED For Apartment Community. 459-4878.
15	ICE CREAM STREET VENDORS WANTED 50% Commission Paid Daily 385-8791

A. Read the new words. Then read the newspaper help wanted ads.

B. Read the questions and write the answers.

1. Write the numbers of the ads that ask for painters.

   _____

2. a. How are the ads for painters the same? _____

   _____

   _____

   b. How are they different? _____

   _____

   _____

3. Roberto wanted a job. It would be his first job. Which of the ads for a painter should he answer?

   _____

   Why? _____

   _____

UNIT 1 Review

A. Write the words below in the sentences.

name	plain	pretty	interest
yes	month	credit	little
so	check	afford	furniture

1. The Popes want to know about _____ rates at this store.

2. They can't _____ to pay all at once for the furniture.

3. Mr. Silva checked their _____ rating.

4. They'll pay a little every _____ for the bedroom set.

B. Write -ain or -ame to make new words. Then write each word in a sentence.

1. sh + ___ = _____   It's a _____ that the Popes couldn't buy the bedroom set.

2. bl + ___ = _____   You can't _____ them for wanting it.

3. m + ___ = _____   A new bed was the _____ thing they needed.

4. str + ___ = _____   Buying a bed now would not put a

_____ on the Popes.

C. Complete each sentence by choosing the correct word.

1. That is the _____ table in the store.
smallest   smaller

2. The Popes have a bed, but they want a _____ one.
newest   newer

3. This bedroom set is the _____ one in the store.
finer   finest

4. "This store could be _____," said Ray.
cleanest   cleaner

UNIT 2 Review

A. Write the words below in the sentences.

farm	their	only	grandmother
wait	price	live	remembers
died	story	off	Ellis Island

1. My grandmother Kate tells us the _____ of her trip to America.

2. She got off the ship at _____ _____.

3. Kate's sister Nell _____ on the ship.

4. Kate _____ her family in the old country with much love.

B. Write -ie or -ice to make new words. Then write each word in a sentence.

1. l + __ = _____   I _____ in bed and listen to Kate's stories.

2. n + ___ = _____   It's _____ to hear her talk about her homeland.

3. pr + ___ = _____   My grandmother paid a big _____ to come here.

4. d + __ = _____   She knew she could _____ on the trip.

C. Write a letter to a friend telling about the story you read.

_____

_____

_____

_____

_____

UNIT 3 Review

A. Write the words below in the sentences.

show	worry	kind	stranger
safe	alone	town	grounds
very	watch	any	project

1. Most parents _____ when their kids are out late.

2. Kim tells Lan and Ming not to go out _____ at night.

3. She says it's not very _____ around here after sundown.

4. We need a guard to _____ the people who come and go.

B. Write *-ound* or *-own* to make new words. Then write each word in a sentence.

1. t + ____ = _____   The project isn't the safest spot in

_____.

2. ar + _____ = _____   People _____ here worry about their families.

3. h + _____ = _____   We'll _____ the owners to make the project safer.

4. d + ____ = _____   We'll go _____ to the meeting room to see the owners.

C. Add *-es* or *-ed* to the word at the left. Write the correct word to complete the sentence.

1. (carry)   The guard at the project _____ a gun.

2. (worry)   Kim _____ if Ming isn't home by sundown.

3. (cry)   When Kim made Lan stay home from a party, she _____.

4. (try)   Kim met with the owners and _____ to tell them about problems in the project.

UNIT 4 Review

A. Write the words below in the sentences.

just	actor	spoil	answer
hard	study	mail	program
real	those	boy	letter

1. *Back Streets* is the _____ Clay likes best.

2. Clay's dad wishes Clay would _____ more.

3. Clay mailed a letter and is waiting for an _____.

4. Rick Reed is an _____ who plays Lucky.

B. Write -*oil* or -*oy* to make new words. Then write each word in a sentence.

1. b + __ = _____   My _____ Clay really likes *Back Streets*.

2. sp + ___ = _____   Rick Reed's letter might _____ *Back Streets* for Clay.

3. t + ___ = _____   Clay is too old to play with _____.

4. t + ___ = _____   Clay has to _____ over his schoolwork.

C. Complete the sentence by choosing the correct word.

1. Rick Reed likes to answer his _____ letters.
    fans'   fans

2. He likes to know the _____ thoughts.
    kids   kids'

3. This _____ job is to play Lucky.
    actors   actor's

4. He shows us what a _____ life is like.
    cops   cop's

UNIT 5 Review

A. Write the words below in the sentences.

call	legal	green	employer
goes	visit	papers	permission
draw	house	American	immigration

1. Pam knew a lot about _____ laws.

2. Rose came to America to _____ her sister.

3. Now Rose would like _____ to work in America.

4. She will need legal help to get a _____ card.

B. Write -all or -aw to make new words. Then write each word in a sentence.

1. s + __ = _____ When Rose _____ America, she wanted to live here.

2. sm + ___ = _____ Rose could get a job working with

_____ children.

3. c + ___ = _____ Pam will _____ the immigration people.

4. l + __ = _____ The _____ says that Rose must get a green card.

C. Complete each sentence by choosing the verb that tells about the past.

1. Rose _____ a long letter to Pam.
   write   wrote

2. Pam _____ the letter to read again later.
   kept   keep

3. She _____ back the tears as she thought of her sister.
   fought   fight

4. Pam _____ it would be a long time before she saw Rose again.
   know   knew

UNIT 6 Review

A. Write the words below in the sentences.

girl	far	idea	noticed
few	true	open	please
wished	warm	start	birthday

1. Pedro liked the _____ of getting to know Ana.

2. He _____ that he could think of a way to meet her.

3. He hoped that giving Ana a card would _____ her.

4. Ana _____ that Pedro was very shy around her.

B. Write -ue or -ew to make new words. Then write each word in a sentence.

1. bl + __ = _____   Pedro was feeling pretty _____.

2. cl + __ = _____   He didn't have a _____ about how to please Ana.

3. n + __ = _____   He bought a _____ card for Ana.

4. gr + __ = _____   Pedro _____ bolder after Ana talked to him.

C. Complete each sentence by choosing the correct pronoun.

1. Pedro asked _____ what to do to meet Ana.
   himself   myself

2. "If she walks home by _____, she might want some company,"
   themselves   herself
   he thought.

3. "Do you want to be by _____?" he asked shyly.
   himself   yourself

4. "I was going to walk home by _____," Ana said, "but I would
   myself   ourselves
   like it if you walked with me."

UNIT 7 Review

A. Write the words below in the sentences.

born	fast	color	creative
done	marks	under	buildings
art	full	paint	neighborhood

1. Pablo lives in a building in this _____.

2. He studied _____ when he was in school.

3. He knows how to be _____ with paint.

4. He wants to make the _____ in his neighborhood look better.

B. Write -ark or -orn to make new words. Then write each word in a sentence.

1. l + ____ = _____   These kids mark up walls as a _____.

2. w + ____ = _____   We're _____ out from trying to stop them.

3. sp + ____ = _____   Pablo wants to _____ some interest in art.

4. sc + ____ = _____   We hope the kids don't _____ his idea.

C. Add -es to the words. Then write the correct words in the sentences.

bus _____   teach _____

wish _____   watch _____

1. Pablo _____ many kids how to paint.

2. He _____ as they make old buildings look new.

3. Pablo _____ he could help all the neighborhood kids.

4. Then they wouldn't mark up the _____ anymore.

Word List

Below is a list of the 314 words that are presented to students in *Book 5* of *Reading for Today*. The numeral following each word refers to the page on which the word is introduced to students.

A

actor	45
address	41
afford	3
afraid	82
ahoy	49
alone	33
American	60
annoy	49
answer	47
any	32
apartments	97
art	89
ate	64

B

babied	36
bark	90
beverages	83
birthday	74
blame	6
blew	77
blind	21
boil	48
book	77
born	87
bosses	92
box	92
boxes	92
boy	46
boycott	49
braid	7
brain	6
bright	21
broil	48
brook	77
brought	64
brow	35
brown	34
building	87
buses	92

C

call	61
carried	36
carries	36
cart	91
chain	6
channel	55
chart	91
check	4
chew	76
choice	49
claw	62
cleaner	8
cleanest	8
clerk	82
clown	34
clue	76
coil	48
coin	49
color	89
continue	96
cool	77
cork	91
corn	90
coy	48
creative	89
credit	4
crew	76
cried	36
crook	77
crown	34
curse	91

D

dark	90
dice	20
died	19
discovered	96
disloyal	49
done	88
drape	7
draw	61
drew	64
drove	64
drown	34
due	76

E

east	27
Ellis Island	19
emergency	41
employ	49
employer	60
experienced	97
extras	83

F

fall	62
far	75
farm	17
fast	87
female	69
few	74
fix	92
fixes	92
flaw	62
flue	76
foil	48
fork	91
form	69
fought	64
frame	6
fright	21
frown	34
full	88
furniture	3

G

gain	6
girl	73
glue	76
goes	60
grandmother	17
grape	7
grasses	92
green	59
grew	76
grounds	32
grow	35

H

hard	46
herself	78
high	21
himself	78
hoist	49
hook	77
horn	90
hound	34
hour	55
house	60

I

idea	74
immigration	59
information	69
insurance	13
interest	5

J

jaw	62
joy	48
joyful	49
just	45

K

kept	64
kind	33
knew	64

L

lark	90
least	83
legal	61
letter	47
library	27
lie	20
little	3
lĭve	18
līve	21
loyal	49

M

maid	7
mail	47
main	6
male	69
marks	88
menu	83
middle	69
minute	55
month	5
mood	77
moon	77
mound	35
myself	78

N

name	4
neater	8
neatest	8
neighborhood	87
nice	20
noise	49
noon	77
north	27
noticed	73
number	41